BAD PETS

TRUE TALES OF MISBEHAVING ANIMALS

ALLAN ZULLO

Scholastic Inc.

New York Toronto London Auckland
Sydney Mexico City New Delhi Hong Kong

To Annika Sofia Wartowski and her sister Clara Annelise,
who certainly will behave better than the animals in this book . . . I hope.
—A.Z.

ISBN 978-0-545-20643-3

Copyright © 2010 by The Wordsellers, Inc.
All rights reserved. Published by Scholastic Inc.

SCHOLASTIC and associated logos are trademarks
and/or registered trademarks of Scholastic Inc.
Lexile is a registered trademark of MetaMetrics, Inc.

15 14 13   12 13 14 15/0

Printed in the U.S.A.   40
First Scholastic printing, September 2010

CONTENTS

WILD AND CRAZY

Just like the human race, the animal kingdom has its share of troublemakers and mischiefmakers, scoundrels and goofballs. It doesn't matter if the animals walk on two legs or four, or live on land or in water, you can bet that some member of most species has done something silly or unexpected.

This book is a lighthearted collection of true stories involving mammals and birds—both wild and tame—whose antics have ranged from the absurd to the zany. If these creatures were people, many of their shenanigans would have landed them in jail, like the shoplifting seagull, carjacking dog, and clothes-stealing cat.

You'll read about such outrageous animals as the dog who was caught trying to snatch a book out of a public library, the deer that sent students scattering after it crashed into their classroom, the parrot who had a knack for offending people as they walked to church, the dog who "drove" a garbage truck into the river, the goose that terrorized a neighborhood, and the bears that barged into a restaurant and ate all the food left behind by the fleeing customers.

Whether they bark, meow, or chirp, one thing is for certain: Some animals can be "wild and crazy."

THIEVES

SWIFT LIFT

A bold seagull has repeatedly shoplifted from the same store in broad daylight.

He began his life of crime in the summer of 2007 when he walked through an open door of a convenience store in Aberdeen, Scotland. A few feet from the door, he stopped in front of a rack that held little bags of potato chips and other crispy snacks. With his beak, he snatched a bag of Doritos and waddled out of the shop.

Witnesses thought it was cute and assumed it was a one-time-only theft. They were wrong.

Because the crime was so easy to pull off, the bird shoplifted again and again from the same store. And he always stole the same thing—a bag of Doritos.

"Everyone is amazed by the seagull," shop assistant Sriaram Nagarajan told reporters. "At first I didn't believe a seagull was capable of stealing crisps [chips]. But I saw it with my own eyes and I was surprised. He's very good at it.

"He's got it down to a fine art. He waits until there are no customers around and I'm standing behind the till [register], and then he raids the place. For some reason he only takes that one particular kind of crisps."

The seagull would walk out with a bag of Doritos and trot or fly to a spot about 20 yards away, where he would rip open the package and dump out the chips. Then, like a winged Robin Hood, he would share his booty with other seagulls.

He quickly became so popular that the locals nicknamed him Sam and even started paying for his Doritos so the store would keep carrying the snack. His thefts have been captured on video and seen worldwide on such Internet sites as www.youtube.com.

"He's becoming a bit of a celebrity," said Nagarajan. "Seagulls are usually not that popular but Sam is a star because he's so funny."

BONEHEAD

A pet Siberian husky named Akira pulled off a daring heist in a grocery store in front of surprised employees and customers when she grabbed a rawhide bone and left without paying.

Her canine caper unfolded in the suburbs of Salt Lake City, Utah, shortly before Christmas 2008. The 11-year-old dog liked to roam way too much, so her owners, John and Holly Stirling of the town of Cottonwood Heights, erected an electronic fence and fitted her with a special collar that gave her an unpleasant shock whenever she tried to cross over the fence.

To Akira, a jolt in the neck was a small price to pay for her freedom. So one day she breached the electronic fence and headed off on a journey. She crossed under two freeways and walked for about six miles to Smith's Food & Drug in the town of Murray. No doubt thinking she deserved a special treat for making it that far, she triggered the automatic door and strolled into the grocery store.

Surveillance video clearly showed what happened next. The gray and white dog headed straight for aisle 16, where all the pet food was displayed, and snatched a rawhide bone worth $2.79 from the lowest bin. Then she turned around and hurried toward the entrance, bypassing the checkout counter.

Store manager Roger Adamson told CNN that he confronted the shoplifter before the dog could get out of the store. "I looked at him. I said, 'Drop it!'" Adamson recalled. "I decided I wanted to keep all my fingers, so I didn't try to take it from him. He looked at me and I looked at him, and away he went, right out the front door. I've never seen him shop here before; brand-new customer, didn't even have his Fresh Value card."

Store employee Tracy Jacobson told CNN, "How likely is that? For a dog to walk into a store, go down the pet aisle, get a bone, and walk out?"

After the clean getaway, local station KSL-TV broadcast footage of the crime that was seen in newscasts around the world and on the Internet. But the thief remained at large for six weeks. When KSL ran a follow-up story accompanied by the surveillance video, the Stirlings saw it and immediately knew that their Akira was the shoplifter. So they brought the dog back to the scene of the crime to face the music.

"There's no question. That looks exactly like the dog," Adamson told KSL, which covered the canine confession. That same verdict was unanimous from store employees, who remembered the electronic collar she was wearing. When the Stirlings turned her loose in the store, Akira followed her nose straight to aisle 16, the pet aisle, paying particular attention to the rawhide bones.

Because dogs are not allowed in the supermarket, Akira had to leave after a short visit. But this time, she stopped at the cash register where the Stirlings paid twice—once for a fresh rawhide bone and the second time for the one she stole.

OUTFOXED

A mother fox swiped more than 120 shoes from doorsteps in the German town of Föhren.

For more than a year, the people of Föhren wondered who was stealing the hiking shoes, workman's boots, flip-flops, and old slippers they had left outside by their doors, in their yards, and on their garden terraces at night. It is customary in some international communities not to wear shoes inside the house.

The mystery was solved in June 2009 after a forestry worker discovered a large collection of footwear in a fox's den in the nearby woods. The bushy-tailed culprit was a mama who had a family of cubs. "She's clearly got a thing about shoes," Rudolf Reichsgraf von Kesselstatt, the local count who lives in Föhren Palace, told Spiegel Online. "We found eighty-six shoes in the den and a further thirty-two in a nearby quarry where they like to play. That includes twelve or thirteen matching pairs of shoes.

"The shoes may well be intended as toys for the cubs because there are bite marks made by little teeth on the shoelaces," he continued. "It's impressive that she found the time to steal them in addition to getting food.

"She's probably got more shoes in the den; we didn't want to venture in any further because she's still living there and we don't want to kill her, especially given that she's got cubs. People should simply make sure they take their shoes in at night."

Count von Kesselstatt had the retrieved shoes laid out in his palace so the townsfolk could claim their lost soles.

CAT BURGLAR

During the day, Jack seemed like a lazy, cute black-and-white house cat. But looks can fool you. When the sun went down, he turned into a midnight prowler who stole clothing and personal items—lots of them—from sleeping neighbors.

In a string of thefts that went on for months, the cat burglar just couldn't keep his paws off other people's things. As dawn approached, the one-year-old domestic shorthair would proudly leave the loot he collected overnight on his owner's stoop.

"It started Halloween night in 2008," his owner, Judy Waring of Coeur d' Alene, Idaho, told www.zootoo.com. "I found a feather boa at our deck door, and I didn't know where it came from, so I pitched it. That was followed by a man's leather glove, and I threw that out, too. But then I saved everything else, because I could see it was Jack bringing it home, and I thought it was interesting."

Jack since amassed a considerable collection of garments, including men's briefs, a bikini bottom, a hoodie sweatshirt, designer shorts, hats, T-shirts, and nearly three dozen gloves, as well as other items, such as towels, a stuffed duck, a back brace, a long rope with a hook attached, and a foam neck cushion.

"His personal record is four gloves left at the front door, and two at the back, in one night," Waring said. "I love the guy, so when he sits proudly next to something on the front step or the back deck, I go out and say, 'Jack, how did you know that this is just what I wanted?' He eats it up. He is a nice boy."

Of course, she didn't want to be an accomplice to a thief, so she tried to make amends with the neighbors.

Figuring victims were wondering where their missing things were, Waring hung stolen items on a clothesline in front of her house. She also posted a sign, asking people to take whatever belonged to them. There were so many articles on display that neighbors assumed she was having a yard sale. Many of the items remained unclaimed.

Rather than getting locked up for his thievery, Jack earned nationwide publicity on local TV, www.youtube.com, CNN, and *Good Morning America*.

Waring said that keeping Jack confined at home was out of the question because he loved to roam at night. She explained, "It's in his blood."

GRIN AND BEAR IT

Frankie the tomcat loved teddy bears. He loved them so much that he sneaked into nearby homes and stole nearly three dozen small stuffed animals in 2008.

The two-year-old feline would enter a victim's house through an open window, door, or cat flap in the middle of the night. Then he would swipe a plush toy or animal and bring the stolen item back through the pet door of his home and triumphantly leave it in the same spot in the living room.

"Frankie looks very pleased with himself when he

comes in with these presents," his owner, Julie Bishop of Swindon, England, told the *Daily Mail*. "He's been going out of the house and coming back with all these toys for pretty much as long as he's been allowed out. They're all soft toys for cats. He doesn't really play with them. He dumps them and goes out looking for something else."

One time, rather than bring home another stuffed animal, he showed up with a giant squeaky hamburger.

Wanting to do the right thing, Bishop plastered her town with posters, trying to return the stolen stuffed animals to the rightful owners.

A LOUSE OF A MOUSE

A field mouse that escaped after being captured by an elderly homeowner got even with the man—by stealing his lower dentures and hiding them inside a wall.

The mouse had taken up residence in the home of 68-year-old Bill Exner and his wife, Shirley, in Waterville, Maine, in 2007. When the couple first heard the rodent making scratching sounds in the bedroom wall, they set out a humane trap on the floor, using peanut butter for bait. Sure enough, the mouse was caught. Exner put it in a cleaned-out, gallon-sized pickle jar with plans to drive the rodent out into the country and release it.

"I left the top off the pickle jar—I figured there's no way this guy can get out. But he escaped," Exner told the *Morning Sentinel*. He caught the mouse a second time. "I put the cover on loosely so he could breathe, and he got out again." Exner trapped the mouse a third time only to have it escape once more.

That night, when Exner went to bed, he removed his lower dentures but was too tired to put them in the bathroom as he usually did, so he laid them on his nightstand. The next morning, the false teeth were gone.

He and his wife scoured the bedroom looking for them. "We moved the bed, moved the dressers and the nightstand and tore the closet apart," he told the newspaper. "I said, 'I know that little stinker stole my teeth. I just know it.'"

In a corner behind the nightstand, the couple found an opening in the wall between a baseboard heater and a structure that covered a water pipe. Convinced that the mouse had hidden his dentures on the other side of the opening, Exner called his daughter's fiancé, Eric Holt, for help.

"He brought a crowbar and hammer and he sawed off a section of wood and pulled up the molding and everything," Exner said. "It was quite a job. We pull it out, and he looks down and he goes, 'I don't believe it! There they are!'

"The dentures were inside the wall, lying right there. They were not damaged. The mouse didn't bite them or anything. It's like he was saying 'I'm going to get even with you for putting me in that jar.'"

After learning about Exner's mouse incident from the *Morning Sentinel*, Patrick Faucher, an animal control officer, paid the Exners a visit and confirmed that the droppings in the pickle jar and near the wall were from a field mouse. He said such a rodent is like a pack rat that spirits away seeds and other food.

Faucher told the newspaper that there was more than one mouse in the house, and that the thief probably had an accomplice who helped haul the dentures inside the wall. "It's like in the cartoons—one pushes, one pulls," Faucher said. "They're pretty ingenious in what they do and I'm sure the smell of food on the dentures had something to do with it."

After Exner disinfected his dentures by boiling and then soaking them in peroxide, he set out the trap once again. By now, however, the mouse had wised up and avoided the trap. It also was acting cocky. Sometimes it would appear out of nowhere and just sit and stare at Exner, according to his wife. "He's taunting him," she told the newspaper. "I swear he's taunting him."

Eventually, the peanut butter was too tempting to

resist, and for the fourth time, the mouse was caught in the trap. And so was another one, the suspected accomplice. Exner turned them over to Faucher, who took them for a drive far from the house and released them back into the wild where they belonged.

BOOK CROOK

A golden retriever named Wofford loved a good book. But his fondness for literary works reached an extreme when he tried to steal one from the library, and the case wound up in court.

Wofford, owned by David Viccellio of Norfolk, Virginia, had a thing about books. Because the family liked to read, there were books everywhere in the house. Whenever a guest came over, Wofford would pick up a book with his teeth and hand it to the person. Other times, the book hound would curl up in the corner with a good paperback.

One day in 1993, the dog slipped through a broken slat in the backyard fence and ambled over to the nearby Larchmont branch library. The back door had been left open to catch a breeze, so Wofford trotted inside. Seeing all those books, Wofford couldn't resist taking one.

He grabbed a children's book off a little table and

tried to sneak by the checkout desk, but a librarian stopped him. Being a friendly pooch, Wofford wagged his tail and gave up the stolen book without a growl.

The librarian called the phone number on Wofford's collar, but no one answered. Recalled Viccellio, "When I got home, there was a message on my answer machine that said, 'This is the library. Your dog is trying to check out a book, and he doesn't have a card.' In fact, the librarian left several messages before calling the animal-control people."

When Viccellio finally showed up at the library, authorities were getting ready to take Wofford to the pound. They turned the pet over to Viccellio and handed him a summons to appear in court for having a dog on the loose and not having a dog license.

"I showed Wofford the summons and that got his attention," Viccellio told reporters. "Afterward, he was burying bones out in the yard. I guess he felt we weren't going to feed him if things went badly in court."

When Viccellio appeared in court, Judge William Oast read the details of the case and asked him, "Was the dog trying to take a book out of the library?"

"No, Your Honor," the owner replied. "He wasn't taking it. He was in the checkout line when they found him."

"Well, that's good to hear," said Oast.

The understanding judge didn't throw the book at Wofford. Instead, he dropped the charges against the dog, but ordered Viccellio to pay court costs of $28.

Reading about the wacky case in the local newspaper, students at an elementary school in Virginia Beach, Virginia, figured out a way to keep Wofford from stealing books from the library—they gave him his very own school library card.

FLYING TACKLE

A hungry hawk proved to be a tough old bird that not only stole a fisherman's bait but also took off with his rod and reel.

The victim was Tommy Meeks of Forest Park, Georgia, who was using an expensive new graphite rod and bait-casting reel on a cold, windy day on Florida's Orange Lake. Meeks shivered as he cast out a large shiner, a small fish, hoping a largemouth bass would strike the live bait. At one point, he put down the rod in the boat and breathed on his hands to stay warm.

He looked up and saw a large hawk zeroing in on his bait. The bird went into its attack mode about ten feet above the water with its claws ready to snare the shiner. The fisherman made a quick grab for his rod, but he wasn't fast enough. The hawk clutched the shiner and, because the bait fish was still attached to the hook, jerked the new rod and reel right out of the boat.

"I was stunned," said Meeks. He couldn't believe what he was seeing—the hawk was flying off with his shiner and 30 feet of line trailing down to his rod and reel. The rod skipped along the surface of the lake, sometimes rising six feet in the air, as the hawk struggled to make off with its prey.

When Meeks recovered from his astonishment, he cranked up his outboard motor and took off in pursuit. He wanted his rod and reel back. The hawk had a 200-yard head start, but Meeks closed in on the bird, which by now had flown over a thick patch of lily pads. Each time the rod fell into the water, the big bird would find another burst of strength and drag it out.

Meeks finally brought the boat next to the rod. "I was just fixing to grab it when the hawk veered off and my rod slammed against my boat," he recalled. The fishing line broke, and the triumphant hawk continued on its way with the stolen shiner. Meanwhile, Meek's new rod and reel sank out of sight in the dark water under the lily pads—lost for good.

It was a shame that the thieving hawk couldn't have "spared the rod."

INTRUDERS

LOOKING FOR A BITE

Sandra Frosti was in front of her computer in her bedroom when an intruder entered her Oldsmar, Florida, home late one April night in 2008.

Hearing strange noises, the 69-year-old woman went to investigate. At the other end of her ground-floor one-story condominium, she peeked into the kitchen and gasped. Then she hurried back to her bedroom, slammed the door, and called 911.

"What's going on?" a dispatcher asked.

"There's an alligator in my kitchen!" Frosti exclaimed.

"How long do you think the alligator is, ma'am?"

"It's huge!" Frosti said. "I only saw the first half of

it, and that had to be at least three feet. It was behind the freezer, and I just disappeared."

Not ready to believe that a big alligator had broken into Frosti's house, the dispatcher said, "Are you sure it couldn't be, like, a, uh, iguana or a really large . . ."

"Oh, no, no, no, no!" Frosti replied.

"All right," the dispatcher told her, "we'll get deputies out that way."

When Pinellas County sheriff's deputies entered the house, they took one look at the gator and fled, taking Frosti with them. Then they called professional alligator trapper Charles Carpenter, an agent for the Florida Fish and Wildlife Conservation Commission.

Earlier that night, Frosti's cat Poe had gone prowling outside the house, which was located in an area of canals and ponds inhabited by gators. Poe attracted the attention of an eight-foot, eight-inch, 220-pound alligator. Figuring the cat would make a tasty treat, the creature followed the feline home. After Poe entered a slightly open porch door, the gator crashed through a porch screen and lumbered through an open sliding glass door into the living room. Poe must have figured he was being stalked because he went into hiding. The gator went looking for him and clomped down the hall, ending up in Frosti's kitchen, where moments later the reptile scared the wits out of the woman.

Because of where she lived, Frosti had seen plenty of alligators in her neighborhood. But the reptiles typically were afraid of people and knew their place belonged in the water. They didn't go breaking into homes like this one did.

When Carpenter arrived, he carefully put a rope around the gator's neck. As the agent was throwing a blanket over its head, the gator hissed and lunged at him. It then thrashed about the kitchen, sending a plate crashing to the floor and denting the wall with its head. Finally, the trapper got a loop of wire on the end of a stick around the creature's substantial neck and then duct-taped its snout.

A deputy stood nearby shooting video of the capture and jokingly told the gator, "You have the right to remain silent."

When the huge reptile was subdued, Carpenter asked Frosti, "Wouldn't you like to pet it and see how it feels?"

"Why not?" she replied. "Most people never get a chance to feel a live alligator." She was surprised that the gator's back was hard as a rock, but the sides were soft.

About 1:30 A.M., the trapper finally dragged the trespasser out of the condo. Because the alligator was not afraid of people and would likely keep returning in its quest for a cat snack, it was taken away and destroyed. Its meat was turned into gator steaks while the hide was shipped to Europe to be made into shoes, belts, and bags.

"It's mind-blowing," Frosti said a few days later on *The Today Show*. "I can't believe all of this. I had an alligator in my kitchen!"

TOO MANY APPLES

Fat Boy was a bad boy.

After slipping out of his residence late one night, the 12-year-old horse roamed around way past his curfew. He trespassed into a neighbor's garden, where he gorged himself on so many fermented apples that he became tipsy. When he tried to stagger out of the garden, he toppled right into a swimming pool and couldn't get out.

Normally Fat Boy was a good boy at Trenance Riding Stables in Newquay, Cornwall, England. But on that October night in 2008, he turned into a four-legged delinquent. After escaping from his barn, he broke into the backyard garden of Sarah Penhaligon to eat some of the apples off her fruit trees. But he couldn't resist all the rotting fruit on the ground that had begun to ferment and produce alcohol. He ate dozens and dozens of the decaying apples.

He became so drunk from the fermented apples that he didn't know which way was out. And that was when he tumbled into the shallow end of the pool in the wee hours of the morning. Try as he might, he couldn't get out.

His splashing and neighing woke up Penhaligon, who peered out her window. "When I looked outside I saw this massive animal in the dark," she told reporters later. Referring to a ghostly black panther that allegedly inhabits Cornwall, she said, "I thought the Beast of Bodmin Moor was in the pool. I was terrified, but when I took a closer look, I realized it was a horse.

"I didn't have a clue what to do next. Who do you call when there's a horse stuck in your swimming pool? I dialed 999 [England's version of 911], and they asked which service I wanted. I said I didn't know because I just had a horse fall in my pool and needed help."

While she waited for a rescue crew to arrive, Penhaligon ran down to the pool to keep Fat Boy company. "He looked a bit panicked," she recalled. "He was trying to get out but couldn't manage it and was getting very tired."

She wanted to calm him down. So, unaware that the pony was drunk, she fed him more of the fermenting apples!

A crew from the fire brigade arrived and spent two hours building a set of steps made from bales of hay in the pool. Then, by using several harnesses, they hoisted Fat Boy out of the water.

A spokeswoman for the stables where Fat Boy lived said horses had been known to get "punch drunk" from eating too many fermenting apples. "It's a good thing he's got a lot of bulk, as it kept him warm," she said. "He was checked over by a vet. Luckily, he was fine, except for the hangover he had the next morning."

CRASH COURSE

A male deer, acting as if he wanted to attend school, crashed through a classroom window, causing startled students to duck for cover. He might not have learned much in his brief, unexpected visit, but he certainly taught the kids a lesson in animal behavior.

Deer have often been seen in the nearby woods of Coopersville East Elementary School in Coopersville, Michigan. But none has been so bold as to bust in on a class—that is, until a six-point buck, weighing about

160 pounds, made his dramatic entrance one December afternoon in 2008.

Leslie Vanlet was teaching her third-grade class about, of all things, the behavior of animals when the buck shattered a double-pane window and leaped into the classroom.

"There was this horrific crash and glass shards were flying everywhere and you wonder, 'What in the heck is going on?'" Vanlet told reporters later. "And then you realize that there's a deer in your room, and it's very surreal. It happened so quickly and yet it all seemed like slow motion. This deer was standing there looking at me straight in the eye and I thought, 'Oh my gosh.'"

The buck upended chairs and desks, knocked books off tables, and dragged a set of mini blinds through the classroom. Vanlet remained cool, instructing her 23 stunned students to drop to the floor while the deer bounded around the room.

"He looked at me and I looked at him and I jumped to my left to get out of the way," she said.

When the deer settled down and stood in a corner, the teacher swiftly shuttled the students from the room and closed the door behind her. The animal shook free of the mini blinds before hopping back out the window and running away. It left behind a trail of broken glass, tipped-over furniture, and scattered books, pencils, and paper.

There was only one minor injury. Ten-year-old Drake McKinley had a small cut on his head after the deer accidentally kicked him while the boy sat at his desk. "It jumped over my desk and hit me right here," he told a reporter for WZZM-TV, pointing to a spot just above his ear. "I touched it and saw blood on my hand."

The buck had six points on its antlers when he entered the school, but he left as a three-pointer because half of his antlers broke off in the classroom. "We should mount it on the wall," said Drake.

Although the teacher and students laughed about the intrusion afterward, Vanlet said the deer gave everyone quite a scare. "He was in the classroom for about thirty seconds," said Vanlet. "The longest moment of my life. This is my first year teaching, and I'll never forget this year as long as I live."

Sergeant Fred Rosel of the Ottawa County Sheriff's Department praised Vanlet's calm response to the situation. He added, "We can only hope the deer is a little bit smarter after visiting [the class]."

UNBEARABLE

Bears with a sweet tooth will do anything—including

breaking into homes and restaurants—to get their paws on sugary treats.

Wally and Sharon Friedlander were in the kitchen of their mountain home in Boulder County, Colorado, testing new flavors of their Italian cookies known as *biscotti*. The couple own an online store called Wally Biscotti, which make, sell, and ship the cookies.

One morning in 2009, they created a blueberry-yogurt-flavored biscotti they called Blues Brothers. That afternoon, they left several trays of the crunchy cookies on their kitchen counter below an open window and stepped out.

They returned later that evening and discovered the kitchen window had been damaged, the trays were strewn about, and biscotti crumbs were everywhere. It wasn't hard to determine who the culprit was. The intruder had left a calling card—bear scat.

Fearing the bear might still be in the home, the Friedlanders called authorities and waited outside until deputies from the Boulder County Sheriff's Office arrived. Deputies searched the home and emerged with a bear—Sharon's oversized stuffed teddy bear, which they carried outside as a little joke.

Sharon told the *Colorado Daily* that she expected the bear—and possibly its friends—to return because "now he's had a good experience" eating their biscotti.

After all, she said, "Wally Biscotti are irresistible, even to bears."

Colorado Division of Wildlife spokeswoman Jennifer Churchill told the newspaper that despite plenty of natural food sources, "bears still seek out human food." They can smell food from up to three miles away.

"Bears will eat anything," added Randy Hampton of the same agency. "Bears will do thousands of dollars of damage opening cupboards or a refrigerator. Bears will actually pull out drawers to make stairs to get to upper cabinets."

That same year, another cookie-loving bear sneaked into the kitchen of a cabin at the YMCA of the Rockies in Estes Park, Colorado, while former television anchorwoman Katie Trexler and her family were in a different room.

Hearing noise, Trexler went into the kitchen and saw the intruder had already opened her Tupperware container of homemade chocolate chip cookies and eaten them all. When the bear saw her, it fled through the same open kitchen window that it had entered minutes earlier.

This was déjà vu for Trexler. Three years earlier, while she and her family were staying in a rented cabin in Snowmass, a bear broke into the kitchen late at night. When Trexler's husband entered the room, there was a bear munching on Trexler's chocolate chip cookies. It's enough to make any cookie baker go "bear-serk."

It didn't matter that a mama bear had no reservations at the Dusty Boot, a restaurant in Beaver Creek, Colorado. She just barged in because of cravings she needed to satisfy.

Employees had seen the bear and her cubs hanging out in front of the restaurant early one evening in 2009. The workers figured that with so many people around, the bears would leave, which they did. What the employees hadn't expected was that the mama would return hours later.

Just before midnight, the bear walked through the open back door and ripped apart boxes containing bags of Pepsi and Dr Pepper syrup used in the restaurant's drink dispenser. "The bear lapped up all the sweet stuff," Johnny Powell, manager and bartender, told the *Vail Daily*.

Once the bear had her fill of the syrup, she headed down the hall to the kitchen, where she encountered a dishwasher. "He spooked the bear just as much as the bear spooked him," Powell said. The bear quickly turned around and left the way she came in.

It's not known whether the unwelcome guest was a relative of a bear that ate a bit too much syrup at a Pepsi-Cola bottling plant in Pueblo 200 miles away in 2001. That weekend, when the plant was closed, a burglar alarm went off inside the building. Police investigated and found paw prints on the floor and puddles of raspberry-tea syrup.

The paw prints led police right to the bear, who apparently drank so much of the sugary liquid that it was sound asleep when it was caught. The animal was tagged and relocated to the mountains near Vail and the Dusty Boot.

NIGHT PROWLER

A masked bandit broke into a federal building in Atlanta and prowled around for several nights, stealing food and snacks from workers' desks.

His crime spree finally ended when he was nabbed in, of all places, a judge's office. Based on the evidence he had left behind—such as distinctive teeth marks on people's food and tiny footprints—authorities were convinced they had caught the culprit.

During the summer of 2008, federal bankruptcy judge Paul W. Bonapfel discovered that a looter had broken into his fourteenth-floor office at the Richard B. Russell Federal

Building and eaten half the apple he had kept on his desk. The perpetrator left a trail of small tracks across a stack of memos.

In the days following the apple caper, other judges and their staffers reported similar crimes, according to the *Atlanta Journal-Constitution*. Chocolate chip cookies were swiped from a desk on the tenth floor. A sandwich was stolen from a drawer in a ninth-floor office. A packet of dried soup was missing from a counter on the twenty-third floor.

The judge gathered employees to help solve the mystery. They photographed the crime scene, took an inventory of missing items, and came to the same conclusion: A raccoon had breached security.

One court clerk designed a "wanted" poster featuring a probable likeness of the intruder. Bonapfel's staff posted a "raccoon crossing" sign on the judge's door.

No one had seen the raider, but there were days when federal employees—who worked in quiet, carpeted rooms—heard him. At different times, strange knocking and squeaking sounds came from the ceilings and walls of offices.

The General Services Administration (GSA), which oversees the building, hired a firm that specialized in catching wildlife. Workers baited a wire trap with tuna and placed it behind ceiling tiles in an office where the bandit was often heard scurrying above.

A few days later, an office worker heard chirping overhead and called for help. Two men climbed a step ladder, removed the ceiling tiles, and collared the suspect, which was indeed a young raccoon. He was promptly named Russell, in honor of the building's namesake, a former Georgia governor and United States senator.

GSA workers believe Russell wriggled into the heating system from outside, then climbed pipes and ventilation ducts that led to various offices where he committed his crimes. The raccoon was found guilty, but the judge went easy on him and sentenced him to probation on a farm far from downtown Atlanta.

PARTY ANIMALS

In what passes as a party in the marine world, 18 obnoxious, noisy, smelly sea lions piled onto an anchored 37-foot sailboat. Like typical 800-pound blubbery creatures, they belched and barked and pooped. They were having a great time. But their fun was cut short—because they sank the vessel.

Gerald Dunlap of Garden Grove, California, had spent two years restoring an antique sailboat that was built in 1910. He named it *Razzle Dazzle* and proudly sailed it along the coast. He kept it moored in the harbor at Newport Beach, which had its share of problems from unwanted flippered guests climbing onto boats.

Over the Labor Day weekend in 2005, deputies from the harbor patrol discovered that a male sea lion had entered the cabin of Dunlap's sailboat. They boarded the craft and forced the trespasser to leave. Unfortunately, it seemed that the sea lion told his buddies what a nice boat it was because two days later, he and 17 other sea lions climbed aboard *Razzle Dazzle*.

Seven tons of blubber was just too much weight for the vessel to remain afloat. It sank in a matter of minutes, ending the sea beasts' bash. Dunlap paid divers $3,500 to raise the boat to the surface. It cost $18,000 more to replace ruined electronic equipment and to make repairs.

Dunlap said that when he learned who sank his boat, "I was kind of dumbfounded."

CAT-ASTROPHE

An ornery orange and white tomcat sneaked into an apartment, dined on fresh fish, and then trashed the place.

While on the prowl in the German town of Itzstedt

36

in 2005, the cat spotted an aquarium in a ground-floor apartment and entered the residence by squeezing through a partly open window. Once inside, he went straight for the big prize—the fish in the aquarium. In his zeal to catch the fish, he knocked the aquarium off its perch, and it shattered on the floor. Now it was easy pickings as the cat gobbled up one little flopping fish after another.

When it was time to leave, he either forgot how he got into the apartment or he was too fat from gorging on the fish to fit through the window. He panicked and went crazy, running around the rooms, tearing down drapes, busting window blinds, and clawing up furniture.

When he heard the tenant enter the apartment, the cat ran and hid before he was spotted. The person screamed in shock over the mess, especially the remains of her little fish strewn on the floor. Convinced that a criminal had trashed her place, she called the cops.

When two officers arrived, they searched the apartment and found the culprit hiding under a kitchen cabinet. But the heavyweight cat resisted arrest, biting one officer on the thumb before he was overpowered.

Now everyone was mad at the feline fiend—the cops, the tenant, and the cat's owner. The police knew who owned the cat because the animal was wearing a collar with a name tag. They took him to the owner, who was ordered to pay for the damage, which was "considerable," a police spokesman told the Reuters news agency.

RASCALS

LUNA-CY

"Help me! Help me!"

Passersby heard a constant cry of what sounded like a frantic woman coming from inside a house in an otherwise quiet neighborhood in Trenton, New Jersey, one September day in 2008. Alarmed by the plea, the people knocked on the door. They failed to get a response other than more cries, so they called the police.

When the officers arrived, they, too, heard shouts of "Help me!" But the front door was locked, and a gate to the fenced-in backyard was chained. Because they spotted a large German shepherd inside, police brought in animal-control personnel. They also called the fire department and emergency medical service. Officers then cut the lock to the gate and kicked in the front door to gain entry and secured the dog.

With guns drawn, police checked the entire house, room by room, from the basement to the roof, in an effort to locate the source of the screaming and a possible suspect. They couldn't find any victim or the culprit.

Just as they were beginning a second search of the house, they once again heard "Help me! Help me!" The cops rushed into the living room and found the screamer—a ten-year-old umbrella cockatoo named Luna. The white, one-pound bird was perched in her cage in the center of the room, astounding police with her pitch-perfect imitation of a woman crying out for help.

Eventually, the bird's owner, Evelyn DeLeon, arrived and could only roll her eyes at all the confusion and excitement that Luna had triggered. DeLeon wasn't surprised to hear that her pet had screamed out for assistance, because the woman had taught the cockatoo the phrase when the bird was six months old. She had trained Luna to yell out for help by taking the pet bird in the shower with her. DeLeon explained to police that she wanted Luna to know the phrase so that if the bird was playing in the yard and a storm approached, she would yell for her owner to come bring her inside before she got wet.

Over the years, Luna increased her ability to shout out words, phrases, and sounds by watching television in both English and Spanish. She became something of a celebrity by serving as the mascot for the local neighborhood watch group.

Her cry for help wasn't the first time that Luna uttered something that brought authorities rushing to DeLeon's house. Seven years earlier, in 2001, the bird cried like a baby for hours. Her wailing spurred neighbors to call officials and report concerns that a baby had been abandoned. When state child-welfare workers arrived at the house, DeLeon showed them that the only baby inside her home was her cockatoo. Luna, she explained, had been practicing the new sound after hearing an infant cry on TV.

Another parrot screaming like a damsel in distress sent police and firefighters rushing to the scene of the "crime."

In 2003, a police dispatcher in Tucson, Arizona, received a 911 hang-up call that apparently was made from a house. When police arrived, they found the home was locked and had bars on the windows. Hearing what they thought was a woman's panicky, screaming voice, police called in firefighters, who used a pry bar and a battering ram to bust down the door.

Police burst into the house and discovered the screams weren't coming from a woman in trouble but from Oscar, a two-year-old yellow-naped Amazon parrot. He was making laughing and screaming sounds as he sat inside his large white cage. "The parrot's screams sounded identical to those of a distressed adult female," said Officer Andrew Davies.

Police asked a neighbor to call Oscar's owner, Dana Pannell, who was at work at the time. Although the identity of the 911 caller remained a mystery, the parrot was seemingly innocent because Pannell's wife, Judy, said Oscar didn't know how to use a phone. She told the Associated Press that Oscar was named after the *Sesame Street* character Oscar the Grouch because of his foul moods.

FLUSHED WITH PRIDE

Two impish cats learned on their own to repeatedly flush the toilet for fun—a trick not much appreciated by their startled owners.

One day in 2001, Russ and Sandy Asbury were alone in their home in Whitewater, Wisconsin, when they heard a toilet flush.

"My eyes got as big as saucers," Russ told the Associated Press. "At first, I didn't know if we had ghosts . . . I couldn't imagine who or what was flushing the toilet."

Sandy went to investigate. She looked in the bathroom and saw her 18-month-old cat Boots standing on the edge of the toilet with his paw on the handle. The couple thought it was a fluke at first, until Boots pressed the handle again and again. Later, their other cat, Bandit, also an 18-month-old, learned to flush on his own—or was taught by Boots.

"We have to shut the bathroom door when we go to bed," said Russ. "Otherwise, one cat or the other is in there flushing away all night."

The cats even started flushing while someone was using the toilet, he added. And they both became skilled at unrolling the toilet paper and turning the bathroom light on and off.

"I've had cats all of my life," Russ said. "But these cats are different than any of the others." He added that the couple's water and sewer bills were getting so high "the cats are going to have to get a job."

In 2002, Charlie, a three-year-old African Grey parrot owned by Zarina France of Ravensthorpe, Dewsbury, England, escaped from his home. The wayward parrot didn't go far, but he began living with a flock of pigeons in the bell tower at St. Mary's Church in nearby Mirfield. No amount of begging or bribery could convince him to return to captivity. He remained free as a bird for several months.

During his days of freedom, Charlie upset the churchgoers—because he liked to let loose with several swear words and wolf whistles at passersby. The vicar received complaints from people who became targets of verbal assault from the bad-mouthed bird.

"Charlie can be very abusive and say all sorts of things that I don't want to repeat," France admitted to reporters at the time.

Church warden Stuart Wooller said Charlie had become a local celebrity. "I have spoken to Charlie several times, and he seems quite happy at the church. I know that he wolf whistles, but I haven't heard him swear at me, probably out of respect because I am the warden."

Yorkshire resident Tim Wood said he was startled after hearing a mysterious voice from above as he walked his dogs in the churchyard. "At first I thought I had really upset someone because of the language that was being used," Wood recalled. "I couldn't believe it when I saw that it was the parrot."

RUDE DUDE

A park in China "sentenced" a mynah bird to 15 days of solitary confinement for being verbally abusive to tourists.

The eight-year-old bird showed up one day in 2005 and made Yuelishan Park in the city of Changsha her home. Keepers at the park named her Mimi, cared for her, and let her have total freedom to roam the grounds. For the first couple of years, she was a crowd favorite, always friendly with tourists.

But then in 2007, after some mischievous visitors taught her some bad words, she began insulting people as they strolled through the park. A park spokesman told the press, "Mynah birds have great imitative skills and can learn to repeat things they hear. We think that tourists taught Mimi swear words. She was saying rude sentences to guests like, 'Hello, big nose,' 'You are ugly,' and 'You are a dimwit.'"

A visitor identified as Mr. Du told the *Chongqing*

Evening News, "I was playing with her and suddenly she said, 'You are a stupid man.' She also called me an ugly man."

After one too many complaints, park keepers captured Mimi and locked her in a darkened cage for two weeks. During her confinement, they subjected her to nonstop recordings of polite conversation in a bid to improve her behavior. They also withheld food from her whenever she uttered a swear word or insult.

Their methods cured Mimi of her habit, and she was once again allowed to wander the park.

"She has been welcoming guests pleasantly," said the spokesman. "Now she has learned to say, 'Hello, gorgeous, you are pretty,' and 'You're a clever boy.'

"If she starts swearing again, she will be caught and played more tapes of polite speech. We hope tourists won't teach her bad language."

RED-CARDED

A pet parrot was thrown out of a soccer match because he kept stopping the action by imitating the referee's whistle.

Irene Kerrigan, 66, had taken her nine-year-old bird, named Me-Tu, to a match between Hatfield and

Hertford Heath in Hertfordshire, England, in January 2009, as she had many times before. The large green parrot always enjoyed watching the game from his perch in his cage, which rested on Kerrigan's lap. He'd never made much noise during soccer matches before.

But during this particular game, play was interrupted several times by a whistle that sounded exactly like the one used by referee Gary Bailey. Each time the players heard the whistle, they stopped playing, even though there had been no foul or injury. Each time, the perplexed referee signaled for the soccer players to carry on. When the whistle kept blowing, Bailey figured that someone in the stands was causing trouble. So he stopped play and marched into the stands to scold the offending fan.

"I was forced to go over to this woman who I thought was making the noises and ask her to stop," Bailey told the *Daily Mirror* later. "But when I confronted her, she said, 'It's not me; it's my parrot.'"

She told him that the bird, who was now sitting quietly in his cage, had never been a problem at other games. She added that Me-Tu enjoyed the fresh air and watching the players from Hertford Heath—his favorite team—run up and down the field. But, unexpectedly, her pet began mimicking the sound of the whistle on this day.

"Every time I blew my whistle, the bird made

exactly the same sound after play had resumed, so the players all stopped," Bailey told the newspaper. "As he grew in confidence, he even started calling out phrases to the players." One of Me-Tu's favorite shouts was "Pretty boy!" directed at any player who ran past him.

In the end, there was only one action the referee could do—give the parrot a red card, which, in soccer terms, means you're kicked out of the game. In this case, Me-Tu was given the boot from the stands. "I didn't have a choice," said Bailey. "I had to send the bird off because it was ruining the game."

After the match ended in a 5–2 win for Hatfield, Hertford Heath's manager, Clive Adlington, said Me-Tu provided a few lighthearted moments for his players during an otherwise disappointing defeat. "It was quite comical, really," he said. "All the lads looking around after hearing a whistle. I'm not convinced [the parrot] would make a very good mascot, mind you."

ARMY BRAT

No dog caused more trouble for an army officer than Riley the fox terrier. He almost got his master kicked out of the service.

Riley was a spoiled, four-legged brat. He was also

the constant companion of Lieutenant Colonel Clarence Deems, commanding officer of the U.S. Army's Fort Howard in Baltimore. A widower, the colonel focused all his affection on his pet dog, allowing the canine full run of the army post, to the annoyance of the other soldiers who were often the target of the canine's bad behavior.

Riley caused such havoc on the post that finally several officers brought charges of incompetence against Deems and tried to get him removed from duty in 1908. The colonel was forced to appear at a War Department hearing to defend himself and his canine companion.

Among the charges leveled against Deems was his lack of discipline of his dog, because Riley:

• would crazily run around the parade ground during marching drills, right through the ranks, barking at the officers and snapping at their heels.

• would eat at the table with the other officers.

• left nasty fleas on the bus that carried officers' wives.

• stole one of his master's boots, forcing the post commander to hobble around for an hour with one foot bootless.

• would lick Deems on the lips while officers were forced to stand at attention.

• would chase certain officers and enlisted men through the barracks.

When it was Deems' turn to testify, he didn't deny any of the charges. However, he went out of his way to praise his canine comrade. "I live all alone, and the dog is a great comfort to me, and I see no reason to be ashamed of it," he said. "I must admit also that he thinks a great deal of me and sometimes jumps all over me. As for being fed at the table, the little fellow has been trained to stand up on his hind legs and beg for a bit of food, and sometimes I do throw him a scrap." He added that at times when Riley ran through the ranks, "I tried to call him back, but he wouldn't come."

When the hearing ended, the army ruled that although Riley was definitely a mischievous dog, he had done nothing seriously wrong—and neither had his master. In fact, two months later, Deems was promoted to full colonel and given a new army post, Fort Hancock. No one was more pleased about the move than the officers at Fort Howard, who would no longer be harassed by Riley.

ALARMING SITUATION

The blackbirds of a small English village learned how to imitate car alarms.

They mastered the alarming trick in 1996 after one bird suspected its territory was about to be invaded, explained David Hirst, a spokesman for the Royal Society for the Protection of Birds. The bird had included the sound of a car alarm into its song, and soon the blaring noise was imitated by dozens of other blackbirds in Guisborough, North Yorkshire, England, creating a daily dawn chorus that jolted residents from their sleep.

Bartender Donald O'Shea told reporters he discovered the phenomenon when he rushed out early one morning to confront what he thought was a car thief, but found only a blackbird in mid-song.

Journalist Mark Topping had a similar experience. "I started hearing this irritating noise outside at five A.M. every day," he said. "It certainly seemed to be a car alarm, but there wasn't one close enough to be making such a noise. Then I saw one particular blackbird sitting in our alder tree, outside the bedroom window. It was giving it everything it had, but instead of the usual pleasant song of the blackbird, it was recreating the din made by a car alarm. After I heard that one bird, I began to realize others had picked it up as well."

The European blackbird—actually a thrush, which is a close cousin of the American robin—can imitate everything from a phone ringing to a cat meowing, said bird-watcher Liz Taylor who lived nearby. She said the blackbirds were enjoying a good joke at the expense of their sleepy human neighbors.

"When I lived in India," Taylor said, "we had a trio of large crows in our garden, one of which could imitate exactly—and in a Scottish accent—my voice calling out for the gardener. When he arrived in response to my summons, the crows would jump up and down on the wall, cackling horribly."

VANDALS

RIP-SNORTING TIME

Barney the guard dog was hired to look after a million-dollar collection of special teddy bears at a British exhibition. It was a job that the six-year-old Doberman pinscher could really sink his teeth into—which is exactly what he did.

While making the rounds one August night in 2006, Barney went on a rampage and attacked dozens of the prized stuffed animals. He ripped, clawed, and chewed rare teddy bears, expensive teddy bears, and historic teddy bears, including the centerpiece of the exhibit. The cuddly bear, called Mabel, was once owned by the King of Rock himself, Elvis Presley, when he was a little boy. It had been handmade in Germany in 1909 and was worth $75,000.

"Up to one hundred bears were involved in the massacre," said Daniel Medley, general manager of Wookey Hole Caves, a tourist attraction in Somerset, England, where the mayhem took place. "It was a dreadful scene."

Barney's mortified handler, Greg West, said, "I still can't believe what happened."

Shortly after he and the dog had arrived for duty, West took the leash off Barney. They walked over to Mabel and stopped. "I was just stroking Mabel and saying what a nice little bear she was," he recalled. Either there was some kind of scent on the teddy bear that switched on the Doberman's deepest instinct to attack, or he was flat-out jealous. No matter. To West's shock, Barney went berserk and tore into poor Mabel, mangling her so badly that her head was left hanging by a thread, and her chest sported a gaping hole.

"Once Mabel had been pried out of his jaws, he went on a rampage," Medley said. "He was grabbing everything in his path, pulling arms off, heads off."

Fur and fluff flew everywhere as Barney savaged bear after helpless bear. It took ten minutes before West could wrestle the Doberman under control. When the slaughter was over, the floor was covered with ruined bears suffering from ripped limbs, gouged eyes, torn-off ears, and tattered tummies. Barney had beaten the stuffing out of nearly 100 teddy bears, some mangled beyond repair.

Mabel will never be the same. She had been loaned to Wookey Hole Caves by its owner, Sir Benjamin Slade, a wealthy Englishman who collected Elvis Presley memorabilia. Just a few months before the attack, he had paid a reported $75,000 for the bear at an auction in Memphis, Tennessee.

Medley, the general manager, had the unpleasant task of phoning Slade and breaking the horrible news. "It was one of the most embarrassing experiences of my life," Medley told reporters. "I had a brief conversation with him, and it's fair to say he was not pleased. I apologized profusely to Sir Benjamin but he just yelled at me. He was absolutely furious. He sent one of his men to collect the body."

Medley faced a second uncomfortable conversation with another private collector who owned dozens of the damaged bears. She was out of the country on vacation when the teddy tragedy occurred. "I hope she doesn't read about [it] in the papers," Medley said at the time, "or she'll be straight back on the next plane."

Ironically, Barney was on duty the night of the attack because the tourist attraction's insurance company insisted upon 24-hour-uniformed security, complete with trained guard dogs, to make sure the expensive bear collection was "one hundred percent secure."

Barney had been a model guard dog for more than six years, according to West. "He's never done anything like this before."

He was never given another chance. Medley said the dog had been stripped of his guard duties and was sent into retirement on a farm "where he can chase chickens."

PRETTY BAD PRETTY BOY

A cockatoo lived up to his gangster name by turning into a destructive hoodlum.

The bird, called Pretty Boy Floyd (named after a pal of notorious mobster Al Capone), became a winged terror when his owner, Mike Gepp, was building a new guesthouse in Nelson, New Zealand, in 2002. The cockatoo chewed up the wiring, wrecked the kitchen, and damaged a nearby car. Not only that, but when he accompanied Gepp into town, the bird tore up leaflets in a bank and stopped traffic by walking in the road.

Pretty Boy Floyd was such a terror that Gepp temporarily banished the bird to an animal sanctuary so he could finish building the guesthouse. "He had to go," Gepp told the local newspaper *The Nelson Mail*. "As fast as we were building, Floyd was pulling it all down."

The cockatoo was kept at Natureland in Tahunanui, where he had been hatched and reared before being adopted by Gepp. But like his gangster namesake, Pretty Boy Floyd tried his best to break out of his confinement. Said curator Gail Sutton at the time, "We keep having to change his cage, because he chews through things."

WIPER SWIPERS

Two crows created havoc for several weeks in 2004 in a parking lot by stripping the rubber off of cars' windshield wipers.

John Foster told BBC Online News he lost six sets of wiper blades after the feathered culprits targeted his car in the Askham Bar Park and Ride parking lot in York, England. He said it took several weeks and several replacement wiper blades on his Ford Mondeo before he figured out what was happening.

"I got into the car one night and was driving home when I realized the rubber was coming off the passenger-side wiper," Foster said. "So I had the blades replaced and three weeks later the same thing happened again." He thought the blades were faulty and put on new ones, but after the third set, he knew something else was wrong.

A little sleuthing pointed to two crows that left a trail of evidence. "I was walking back to my car one evening and noticed four or so bits of rubber on the ground," Foster recalled. "So I went to the park and ride office and the guy said, 'Oh, yes, we know about it. It's crows and we've got them on video.' I was staggered. I just couldn't believe it; I thought it was vandals."

Actually, it was caused by vandals—only they were birdbrains.

A spokesman for the Royal Society for the Protection of Birds (RSPB) had two theories to explain the birds' bizarre behavior. He said the birds could have been attracted by the taste of a component in the rubber. Another possibility: The birds saw their reflections in the windshields and attacked the wiper blades, believing they were rival crows. Whatever the reason, drivers were advised that after they parked their cars they should wrap the wipers in towels to keep the crows away.

Although the two birds were a costly nuisance to the motorists who had to replace their wipers, many locals took a shine to the crows—and even named them

Russell and Sheryl (after actor Russell Crowe and singer Sheryl Crow). When word spread that officials planned to kill the feathered fiends, bird lovers protested. The City of York Council listened and issued a stay of execution. Officials eventually caught Russell and Sheryl and moved them to an area where they wouldn't vandalize cars.

FIRE STARTER

A family dog that either didn't like his owner or didn't like fried fish—or both—shared the blame for causing a fire that severely damaged its owner's house.

One December evening in 2007, Andre Perrault's wife was frying fish in the kitchen of her home in Topeka, Kansas, when she stepped outside to throw away some trash. Her dog had tailed her to the back door. When she reached the garbage cans out back, the dog put his front paws on the door and closed it behind her. When the woman tried to get back in, she discovered that the door was locked. In fact, all the doors to the house were locked . . . and she didn't have a key.

Perrault told the *Topeka Capital-Journal* that he was across town when his wife called on a cell phone to let him know the dog had locked her out of the house while food was frying on the electric stove. Perrault rushed home and gained entry with his key to find a serious grease fire in the kitchen.

Topeka Fire Department Captain Greg Degand said the home's residents had attempted to extinguish the blaze. "They thought they had it out," Degand said. "But it had gone up into the attic."

By the time the fire trucks arrived, heavy smoke and flames were coming out of the attic of the one-and-a-half-story house. It took firefighters about 15 minutes to bring the blaze under control. The fire caused an estimated $50,000 in damage.

Although his wife was upset, Perrault said he was thankful that no one was injured, including their pet bird . . . and the dog that started it all.

IN HOT WATER

A pet parrot that had been left home alone and out of its cage was so bored, it turned on a faucet to amuse itself. The owner wasn't amused—especially after he returned home to a flooded apartment.

According to the Dutch newspaper *Utrechts Dagblad*, Jan Borst of Utrecht, the Netherlands, let his parrot out of its cage and then left it home alone on Christmas in 2001. Several hours later, neighbors in the apartment directly below his called the fire department after they saw water dripping from their ceiling.

When firefighters arrived, they entered Borst's apartment and discovered the tap that was connected to the washing machine had been turned on. The faucet was right next to the parrot's open cage. Borst said the bird sometimes played with the tap, but he never thought the bird could actually turn it on. The flood caused more than $5,000 worth of damage.

HOME WRECKER

At the home of his new owners, a Rottweiler puppy had a blast—one big enough to destroy the house.

Paula Dodson and her family had gone out for the day and left their three-month-old puppy, Jake, alone at their Norman, Oklahoma, house one evening in 2001. When they returned, they were shocked to see that their home had turned to rubble. An explosion had blown the roof six inches off the house and collapsed several brick walls.

Almost as stunning was their discovery that Jake was alive in the middle of all the debris and had suffered only minor injuries. "I can't believe it, and even our vet can't believe it," Dodson told reporters.

Firefighters speculate that Jake was playing with a gas-line switch in the utility room when he accidentally turned it on, filling the room with natural gas. When the hot-water tank switched on, the spark ignited the gas, causing the violent explosion.

A LOT OF BULL

Limousin cattle are known for their muscular bodies, reddish brown color, and easygoing manner. But one Limousin bull brought shame to his breed because he didn't realize that he was supposed to have a calm temperament.

In May 2008, the big brute made up his mind that he no longer wanted to remain with his herd of cattle grazing on a farm near the German town of Monschau. The bull broke through a fence and took off. He could have run to another pasture where the grass was greener, or hooked up with another herd, or found a farm where the accommodations were nicer.

Instead, he chose to invade a nearby house while an unsuspecting family was sitting down for a meal. With no warning, the bull burst through the back door, upended the kitchen table, charged down the hallway, and destroyed most of the furnishings in the living room.

Once the head of the household recovered from the shock of an uninvited rampaging bull in his home, he managed to open the front door as a gesture to the animal that it was time to leave. The hoofed marauder got the hint and left—but not before causing about $16,000 in damages to the house and its contents.

"The animal basically did a tour of the hall, the kitchen, and the living room before leaving," said Paul Kemen, a spokesman for police in the city of Aachen. "It came in the back and went out the front."

Fortunately, no one in the family was injured. The bull was captured and the owner made sure the beast would never again go barging into other people's homes.

A bull that had some issues with a neighbor ran over to the man's house and repeatedly attacked it.

The animal got loose from his fenced-in pasture on a nearby farm one September morning in 2007 in Killingly, Connecticut. Once free, he headed straight for neighbor Wayne Johnson's property and turned into a four-legged wrecking crew.

Johnson happened to be in his yard when the bull showed up and charged repeatedly into the side of the house. As the man watched, dumbfounded, the animal tore off chunks of clapboard siding, flipped over a picnic table, tore down part of the fence around his swimming pool, and then, for good measure, rammed Johnson's car.

"He was crazy," Johnson told the press. "The thing was ripping my house apart."

Johnson called police, but they declined to help. Eventually, a neighbor with a bag of grain lured the bull back to its pasture. Johnson, who demanded that the owner pay for all repairs, said he had no idea what caused the bull to become so aggressive. "My house isn't even red," he said. "It's grayish blue."

HIJACKERS

WATER DOGS

Charlie the Labrador stole his master's car, but he didn't get far—because he drove it straight into the river.

And guess what? He wasn't the only canine to drive a vehicle into the water.

Charlie was one of those challenging pets who had been in the "doghouse" many times for his destructive habits of chewing on furniture, knocking over water glasses, and snatching food from the kitchen table. But because of his sweet disposition and silly antics, the family always forgave him.

It took all of the forgiveness they could muster

for the stunt he pulled one June evening in 2007 at his home in Sagle, Idaho. Charlie was waiting for his owner, Mark Ewing, to come home from picking up pizza for the family. When Ewing showed up, the dog jumped around happily to greet him. As Ewing walked toward the house, Charlie jumped into the open window of his master's Chevy Impala that was parked in the driveway.

As if showing off his limited driving skills, Charlie knocked the gear selector into neutral and then barked as the car rolled down the sloping driveway and straight for the Pend Oreille River on the other side of the street. Apparently realizing that the car had no business being in the water, Charlie leaped out the window and galloped back toward the house while the car crossed the street and plunged straight into the river.

Ewing, meanwhile, just stared in disbelief as he watched the Chevy sink below the surface. He told the Spokane *Spokesman-Review*, "There's nothing weirder than looking at your car cruising down your driveway when you're not in it and seeing your dog jump out and then watching your car go splash."

A Newfoundland named Bear pulled a similar caper—only with a garbage truck.

The Newfie is a breed of dog known for its giant size,

gentle manner, and swimming ability. It is not, however, known for its skill at operating a vehicle.

Apparently, Bear wasn't aware of this limitation.

Early on a winter morning in 2001 in Greenville, New Hampshire, Glen Shaw, the operator of a local trash-collection service, decided to let his huge three-year-old canine pal accompany him on his garbage rounds. The dog gleefully leaped into the cab of the ten-wheeled trash-compactor truck and sat quietly in the passenger seat.

At one stop, Shaw stepped out to collect the trash, as he had done several times that morning. But this time, Bear moved over to the driver's side ... and that was when the excitement began. As Shaw was loading garbage into the back of the truck, Bear somehow released the hand brake. Because the vehicle had been parked on the downward side of a small hill, it began rolling forward. That was bad enough. But even worse, the street dead-ended at the Souhegan River.

Shaw chased after the truck, but it was gaining so much speed and momentum that he couldn't catch up to it. Behind the wheel, Bear saw his master growing smaller in the sideview mirror. The dog should have been paying more attention to what was in front of him.

The truck smashed through the guardrails at the

end of the street and landed nose-first in the river below. Bear was unharmed but understandably agitated by his first attempt at operating a truck, now that water was seeping into the cab. Although he knew how to swim, he didn't know how to get out of the vehicle. Fortunately, his master jumped into the river in time to get him out.

Later, Shaw's wife, Ann, told the *Union Leader & New Hampshire Sunday News*, "My husband said that's [Bear's] last ride in the truck."

HOLD-UP BIRD

A pet parrot single-wingedly hijacked a commercial plane, preventing it from taking off after she flew throughout the cabin and nipped at the frightened passengers.

Polly the parrot was sitting on the lap of her owner, one of 18 people in the cabin of the Aurigny Air Services Trislander aircraft as it was getting ready to leave the British island of Alderney for Southampton in June 2006. "There was a bit of a problem with Polly," duty officer Steve Roberts told the British tabloid *The Sun*. "Her owner was taking her away on holiday, and I think she just got a bit excited."

As the plane was taxiing down the runway for

takeoff, the parrot managed to get free. The bird flew through the cabin, circling passengers' heads and pecking their shoulders. Some people were screaming at her while others were shouting at the pilot to stop the takeoff.

Once he realized what all the commotion was about, the pilot turned the plane around on the runway and taxied back to the gate. The crew emptied the cabin of the passengers and cornered Polly. They scooped up the gray and white parrot and put her back in her box. Then they received assurances from her owner that the bird would remain confined for the duration of the flight.

After a ten-minute delay, the passengers got back on the plane. "Polly was quite happy," said Roberts. "She was very good-natured, really."

One passenger told *The Sun*, "To be honest, it was very funny looking back after the event. But if the flight had been in midair and the bird had been pecking the pilot, it could have been dangerous."

Roberts said the airline took the attempted hijacking in stride. "We deal with all sorts of things here." He called Polly's hijacking attempt "a bit of unscripted in-flight entertainment."

Bentley the mutt ended up in a drive-in that had nothing to do with food.

On a frigid November night in 2008, the 50-pound boxer/Shar-Pei mix went with his master, Bryan Maher, to Cool Beanz, a coffee shop in the town of St. James on Long Island, New York. Maher, a singer-songwriter, parked his 1992 Ford van and went inside to sign up for open-mike night. He left the vehicle running because, he later told the *New York Daily News*, "it was cold outside, and I didn't want my dog to freeze."

The five-year-old dog had formed a strong bond with Maher, who had adopted him from the pound a month earlier after learning that his previous owner abused him. So when Maher left him in the van for just a couple of minutes, Bentley couldn't stand it. He jumped behind the steering wheel and, seeing his master through the coffee shop's front window, began pawing at the windshield because he wanted to be with him.

Bentley got his wish.

After accidentally knocking off the rearview mirror from the windshield, Bentley jostled the gearshift lever from park into neutral. The vehicle rolled forward down an incline, smashed into the store's patio furniture out front, and then struck the window, badly cracking it. The van suffered a few dents and scratches. Fortunately no one was injured.

Maher was talking to the shop's owner, Patricia McCarthy, when he happened to look up and see his van heading straight for the front window. "The next thing I knew, I saw my van coming at me with Bentley in the driver's seat grinning at me," Maher recalled. "It was like he was saying, 'Here I am!' He was as happy as can be."

Despite the damage, neither Maher nor McCarthy could get mad at Bentley. "Bentley was wagging his tail afterward," said McCarthy. "He really is a sweet dog."

Maher was grateful to McCarthy for taking it all in stride. She gave him a free cup of coffee and even booked him for open-mike night.

Maher said he had learned his lesson. "This is the first and last time I'll ever put the van in park and leave it idling," he said. To make sure his canine companion would stay warm, Maher bought him a nice doggy coat for Christmas.

"He's a smart dog," Maher added. "Obviously, he can drive a van."

No, obviously he can *crash* a van.

TREE-MENDOUS MISTAKE

A dog named Rancher locked his owner out of a pickup, put it in gear, and drove the vehicle into a tree.

It happened when Lyle Sneary brought his dog with him to check on cattle after a snowfall in February 2002 on his 1,200-acre farm near Alva, Oklahoma. Sneary stopped the 1993 Dodge pickup after he spotted a downed cow that had recently given birth.

Sneary, 67, later said, "I got out to tend to the cow, but I left Rancher inside. I had turned off the engine, put it in park, and rolled the window down about four inches. I was about twelve feet from the truck and giving the cow some feed. Some cows saw this and figured that maybe she was getting something better than they were, so they wandered over toward the front of the pickup.

"When they got close, I hollered at them to get away. Well, when he heard me holler, he thought that meant he needed to come unglued. He jumped up against the door on the driver's side and hit the automatic button that locked it. But I didn't know it at the time.

"Then he kept barking and leaped on the dashboard and knocked the gearshift lever out of park and into neutral. The pickup was parked on the downward slope of a little hill. When I saw the truck rolling downhill, I chased after it and jumped on the running board.

"I tried to open the door but it was locked. Then I stuck my arm in the opening in the window, trying to unlock the door so I could get to the steering wheel, but I couldn't quite reach the lock. The pickup was gathering more speed. For some reason, the vehicle made a little bit of a left turn and headed right for a tree. Whether Rancher turned the steering wheel, I can't say because I was so busy. All I know was he was sitting in the front seat watching all of this.

"The tree was coming up real fast, so I bailed out, and the pickup rammed into that tree real hard—hard enough where the insurance company declared it a total loss."

Fortunately, Rancher was not hurt. Unfortunately, his owner was angry at him. "I was so doggone mad at him that I wouldn't let him out of the pickup," he said. Sneary had to trudge a mile and a half in the deep snow in freezing temperatures to a shed where he had left his cell phone. When he reached the shed, he called his wife to come and get him.

Eventually, Sneary forgave his dog. "Rancher is a good dog, just like his daddy, Farmer, was," he said. "Every time I go out to check the cows, Rancher goes with me. And for safety reasons, I let him ride up front rather than in the back of the pickup. He's saved me a thousand miles of walking when I've got cows out.

"And he's saved my hide many times when I come into town after dark because in my area there are a zillion deer, and about every week someone runs into a deer and smashes up their vehicle. That dog stands attentive, and even when it's dark, he'll alert me that there's something out there, and I slow down. He sees what I don't see."

When word of Rancher's escapade spread, Sneary took a lot of ribbing from friends, including Oklahoma Highway Patrol Trooper Chris West. Recalled Sneary, "He called me and said, 'I'm going to have to revoke Rancher's driver's license.'"

AIR SCARE

A bald eagle forced down a commercial jetliner.

It all started innocently in 1987 near Juneau, Alaska. The eagle dived and snagged a salmon out of a river and flew off toward its nest, called an *aerie*, with the tasty fish clutched in its talons.

Just then, the eagle spotted a giant silver bird heading toward it from below. The frightened eagle decided it was best to dump its prey and flee for its life. The salmon fell through the air and slammed into the cockpit window of the bigger bird—an Alaska Airlines Boeing 737 that had just taken off from Juneau. Fortunately, the window didn't break.

Still concerned about possible damage, the pilot of the Anchorage-bound jetliner made an emergency landing in Yakutat, 200 miles away, where mechanics made a careful inspection. "They found a greasy spot with some scales, but no damage," said Paul Bowers, the Juneau airport manager.

The flight's 40 passengers were forced to cool their heels for about an hour before the plane was pronounced airworthy and allowed to continue on to Anchorage.

The bizarre incident went down in aviation history as the first-ever midair collision between a commercial jetliner and a fish. The eagle apparently escaped injury, but was no doubt keeping a close eye on those bigger, noisier birds.

DOGGONE IT!

Max the boxer had a license, but it wasn't the kind that gave him the right to drive off in his master's truck, which is exactly what he did.

Charles McCowan of Azusa, California, was driving his pickup with his canine buddy sitting next to him in the front seat when he made a stop at a mini-mart one day in 2008. McCowan put the gear selector in neutral and applied the emergency brake before leaving Max in the truck and going into the store.

The 80-pound boxer just couldn't pass up an opportunity for a little fun. As he moved along the front seat, he hit the brake lever. With the pickup in neutral, the vehicle began to roll backward on the slanting parking lot. The truck headed out of the lot, across four lanes of traffic, and into the parking area of a fast-food restaurant across the street.

Imagine McCowan's surprise when he stepped out of the store and discovered that both his truck and his dog were missing. Assuming the pickup had been stolen, he called the police. Shortly after showing up, the officers looked across the street and spotted the vehicle and its unlikely driver. Both dog and truck didn't have a scratch on them.

Just to confirm that the dog had indeed "driven" the pickup across the street, the police studied security video from the store. And doggone if it didn't show Max in the driver's seat as the truck rolled backward into the street. Luckily, Max managed to miss running into other cars before the vehicle came safely to a stop in the other lot.

Other than suffering the bad feeling of thinking his

truck and dog were stolen, McCowan said things could have been much worse. "I was just thinking of the trouble Max could have caused," he told the press. "The pickup could have hurt somebody; the timing had to be just perfect to avoid hitting other vehicles."

FRIGHT FLIGHT

A pit bull who did not like flying created chaos in the cargo hold of a commercial jetliner as it flew clear across the country.

The dog, whose name was not made public, had been placed in a cage by his owner and loaded into the cargo hold of an American Airlines Boeing 757 for a flight from San Diego to New York in 2002. The pit bull was upset with his accommodations and began clawing and gnawing on the cage.

At some point during the flight, the dog finally worked himself free and slipped out of the cage. Then he took out his anxiety on the plane itself.

Crew members said they heard thumping noises coming from the cargo hold and discovered that backup radio and certain navigational equipment weren't working. They couldn't figure out why until the plane landed safely in New York. When ground crews opened the cargo hold doors, they spotted the pit bull running free. The dog had gnawed a hole in the bulkhead, damaged the cargo-hold door, and chewed through garden hose–sized electrical cables.

The damage was so severe that it knocked the plane out of commission for repairs for nine days. Despite all the harm the dog had done, an airlines spokesman said the plane and its passengers were never in any danger.

However, after the incident, American Airlines announced it was banning all potentially aggressive dogs from its planes. The airline said the ban was a matter of safety and would apply to all pit bulls, Rottweilers, Doberman pinschers, and any other dog that exhibits aggressive behavior.

DRIVING BEAR-FOOTED

A bear smashed its way into a minivan, gobbled up a bag of Halloween candy that was inside, and then took the vehicle for a joyride before dumping it on the side of the road and fleeing into the woods.

In 2007, an officer in Vernon, New Jersey, was patrolling the Highland Lakes section at 2 A.M. when he found a 2004 Mazda minivan parked at an odd angle on the shoulder of the road. The vehicle's front passenger-side window was smashed. Upon further investigation, the officer discovered plenty of clues that pointed to a big, hairy suspect. There were paw prints on the windshield, gobs of drool on the cloth interior, claw marks on the door panels, and black hair on the seats, not to mention candy wrappers everywhere.

The officer concluded that earlier in the night, the bruin was snooping around the minivan, which was parked in the driveway. The animal broke into the vehicle after it spotted a bag of Halloween candy that had been left on the front seat. While gobbling up the goodies, the bear dislodged the parking brake, causing the minivan to roll down the sloping driveway and onto the road. The beast then "drove" the vehicle in reverse for about 40 feet before the Mazda came to a stop off the road.

In a tongue-in-cheek press release titled "Black Bear Goes for a Joyride," the police department said the officer "followed the candy-wrapper trail into the woods, but was unable to locate the defendant black bear."

Detective Sean Talt told the *Star-Ledger*, "We've had animals break into houses, but this is the first time we've ever had an animal take the car like that."

RAISING A STINK

A skunk sneaked on board a commercial jetliner and created such a smelly situation that it grounded the plane for a couple of hours.

At Miami International Airport, baggage handlers were loading an American Airlines plane bound for Bogotá, Colombia, one afternoon in June 2008 when they discovered a skunk in the back of the cargo hold. Since it didn't have a ticket, they tried to kick the stowaway off the plane.

Even though the critter was outnumbered, it wasn't going to leave without raising a stink. And being a skunk, it did what any red-blooded American skunk is supposed to do when threatened or cornered. It discharged its disgustingly foul odor.

The awful stench didn't just overpower the baggage handlers. It was so strong that the smell spread to the cabin, where the passengers were settling into their seats. Needless to say, the passengers were not willing to remain seated, now that they were holding their noses and gagging. The flight attendants quickly ushered everyone off the plane.

Meanwhile, an airport employee managed to safely remove the skunk from the plane and transport it to another location. An airline spokesman said no one could figure out how the critter managed to sneak aboard without being spotted. Although the skunk had been taken away, it still took more than two hours before the crew could get rid of the rotten smell in the cabin and cargo hold.

In a classic understatement, the airline spokesman said, "It smelled real bad in there."

THUGS

TONGUE-TIED

There was no way a snapping turtle was going to let Calvin Embry kiss him, so it latched onto his tongue and wouldn't let go.

For the next few weeks, Embry was talking a little funny.

Embry, 41, a laborer and turtle hunter from Wayne City, Illinois, was at a local fireworks event on the Fourth of July 2008 when one of his buddies asked Embry to show everybody how he could hypnotize a snapping turtle and kiss him right on the snout.

"I started doing this trick years ago, and it's a great crowd pleaser," Embry told the *Evansville Courier &*

Press. "I guess I've kissed about a hundred snappin' turtles and never been bit—until this last time."

Embry took a 15-pound snapper out of his truck and then tried to hypnotize the turtle by tilting it at a certain angle and rubbing its belly. "If you do it just right, they get all relaxed and everything and you can kiss 'em right on the snout," he told the paper.

Like he had done many times before, the turtle man went through the routine flawlessly, convinced that the snapper was asleep. But this particular turtle was in no mood to be hypnotized, let alone kissed, by a human.

The reptile latched onto Embry's tongue as he was preparing to lick its eyeballs. "When it happened, everybody started running around like crazy and were yelling," Embry said. "Do you know how hard it is to talk with a fifteen-pound snappin' turtle hanging off the end of your tongue?"

Embry finally was able to communicate to a friend to pry open the turtle's mouth with a knife, which he did. When the turtle finally let go, Embry went to the emergency room where a doctor treated what was left of the front of his tongue.

"That doctor hadn't ever seen anything like this, so he took some pictures for the Southern Illinois University School of Medicine," Embry said. "I got a tetanus shot and he sent me home."

Even though he was missing a chunk of his tongue, Embry insisted he would continue to kiss snapping turtles on the snout and lick their eyeballs. And what about the snapper? "I kept that old turtle," said Embry, "and will probably have him mounted by a taxidermist one of these days."

SERVING TIME

Blacky the donkey spent three days in the same jail used to lock up human criminals after he was charged with assault and battery.

According to police in Tuxtla Gutierrez, Chiapas, Mexico, the donkey was grazing outside a ranch when he attacked two men in May 2008. Blacky bit a 63-year-old man in the chest and then stomped on and broke the ankle of another man who had come to the rescue. It took six men to control the donkey. No reason was given why the animal assaulted the victims.

But police had all the reason they needed to throw Blacky into the slammer that normally held petty criminals. "Around here, if someone commits a crime, they are jailed," Officer Sinar Gomez said, "no matter who they are." Or in this case, what they are.

After three days behind bars, Blacky was released

because his owner, Mauro Gutierrez, paid a $36 fine and the $115 hospital bill of the victims. Gutierrez also agreed to pay $480 to each man for the days they missed work because of their injuries.

This wasn't the first time that Chiapas police had arrested an animal and tossed it in the pokey. Earlier in the year, a bull was put behind bars after police received complaints from residents of the town of Canalumtic that the beast devoured their corn crops and destroyed two wooden vending stands. In 2006, a dog was locked up in jail for 12 days after biting someone.

LOOSE GOOSE

A hot-tempered goose terrorized a neighborhood, chased a pet dog, and briefly trapped a woman in her house.

The winged mugger showed up one morning in 2008 on a quiet street in Chico, California, and flew into a rage. It charged after people, who had to scurry indoors to avoid its wrath.

Susie Tambe told the local newspaper *Enterprise Record* that she heard the goose honking about 8 A.M. and went outside with her dog, Jade, to investigate. They walked around a pickup truck in a neighbor's driveway when they were confronted by the large bird. The goose began chasing the dog, which then sprinted down the street and ran back toward Tambe with the bird in close pursuit. Tambe and Jade then scampered into the backyard and she slammed a gate behind them.

Minutes later, Tambe went to the front door and saw the goose waddling up the walkway toward her. She told the paper that although she felt fairly safe inside, the goose made it impossible for her to leave her home. The bird kept lunging at the screen door. Whenever any neighbors came near Tambe's home, the goose flapped its wings, honked, and charged them.

Someone called the police. Among the cops who arrived was Sergeant Linda McKinnon, the officer best suited to collar this feathery fiend because she had pet geese at home. The police tried to corner the goose in Tambe's yard by herding it with a broom.

Eventually, McKinnon grabbed the bird, carried it to her patrol car, and locked it in the backseat. Animal-control officers took custody of the goose, which wasn't injured, and turned it over to the Bidwell Wildlife Rehabilitation Group.

Spokeswoman Marilyn Gamette told the newspaper that the goose was probably someone's pet. She tried to release it at a wildlife refuge outside of town, but the bird immediately flew back and landed at her feet. Gamette was able to successfully release it later at another nature area where several other half-domesticated waterfowl resided.

Why was the goose behaving so badly? Gamette told the newspaper, "It was probably just looking for a handout."

BITING STATEMENT

President George W. Bush's dog Barney was in hot water for biting White House visitors, including one whose attack was captured on video.

In November 2008, Reuters TV White House correspondent Jon Decker spotted the president's black Scottish terrier on a morning walk on the North Lawn. Decker reached down to pet the dog, but Barney snapped and bit the reporter's right index finger. April Ryan of American Urban Radio Networks happened to capture the moment on video. And, naturally, it wound up on www.youtube.com. The video comes to an end with a freeze-frame on Barney's fangs.

The bite broke skin, causing enough bleeding to prompt White House physician Dr. Richard Tubb to treat Decker with antibiotics. The reporter also had to get a tetanus shot.

"I think it was Barney's way of saying he was done with the paparazzi," said Sally McDonough, a spokeswoman for First Lady Laura Bush. At Mrs. Bush's request, McDonough called Decker to make sure he was fine. She said that Decker was "being a good sport about it all."

According to ABC News, Barney had a history of biting. On West Wing White House tours, visitors were not permitted in the Rose Garden whenever Barney was outside because he had bitten guests.

Boston Celtics public relations director Heather Walker said that Barney bit her wrist and drew blood as she tried to pet him after a White House ceremony honoring the team's seventeenth NBA championship. "It was very strange. I didn't expect him to bite me," Walker said.

She did not get any injections because, she said, Barney was well cared for. "I was told that he doesn't like people in the media and press," Walker joked.

EXTREME SCHEME

Santino is not your average chimpanzee. He's got a chip on his shoulder and hurls rocks at visitors of the Furuvik Zoo in Sweden where he lives. What sets him apart from other chimps isn't that he behaves so badly; it's that he plots his attacks well in advance.

Since 1994, the cunning chimp has spent his mornings gathering ammunition for his weapons cache. Before the zoo opens, he typically collects rocks from the bottom of the moat that surrounds his man-made habitat and stores them in piles on the side of the island that faces the zoo's visitors. He also hacks pieces of concrete from the artificial rocks at the center of his enclosure and adds them to the piles.

As the dominant male of the zoo's other chimps, Santino then patrols the area in a calm, deliberate manner. But usually in the early afternoon, he undergoes a change and starts harassing guests with the rocks that he had collected earlier in the day.

Zookeepers have tried to stop Santino's attacks with little success. Says Mathias Osvath of Lund University, who has studied the rock-throwing chimp, "Sometimes [the caretakers] will keep him in during the morning, and only let him out once the visitors have arrived. It's very hard to stop him because he can always find new stones, and if he can't find them, he manufactures them. It's an ongoing cold war."

The attacks are never directed at chimpanzees, but only at humans viewing the animals from across the moat.

However, "Santino rarely hits visitors because of his poor aim," said Osvath. In the few instances where his rocks have struck someone, the person was not injured.

Osvath said the chimpanzee had also been observed tapping on concrete boulders in the park to identify weak parts and then knocking out a piece. If it's too big for throwing, he breaks it into smaller pieces before adding them to his arsenal.

"It is very special that he first realizes that he can make these and then plans on how to use them," Osvath said, adding that Santino might be considered a genius in the chimpanzee world because he plots his attacks for the future.

Researchers who have studied Santino think he launches his salvo of rocks at visitors because he wants to feel powerful. "It is extremely frustrating for him that there are people out of his reach who are pointing at him and laughing," said Osvath. "It cannot be good to be so furious all the time."

AIR RAID

Two eagles, miffed that someone had invaded their territory, tried to knock Britain's top female paraglider out of the sky.

It happened when Nicky Moss, 38, was sailing at an altitude of about 8,000 feet during competition at the 2007 Killarney Paragliding Classic over the outback southwest of Brisbane, Australia.

She was harnessed under her 38-foot-wide parachutelike canopy, or wing, while riding a thermal (a rising current of warm air). Suddenly, she was attacked by two wedge-tailed eagles. Possessing a wingspan of nearly seven feet and razor-sharp talons, eagles are Australia's largest birds of prey and sometimes called the sharks of the sky.

"I heard screeching behind me and an eagle flew down and attacked me, swooping down and bouncing into the side of my wing with its claws," Moss told Reuters. "Then another one appeared."

The pair of eagles began circling her in a coordinated attack. First, one peeled off and zoomed at her from behind; then the other came in from a different angle, tearing at the wing and poking holes in it. Rips in the top made the glider harder to control, so Moss began a corkscrew descent. But the eagles continued to attack her.

"One of them swooped in and hit me on the back of the head, then got tangled in the glider which collapsed it," she recalled. "So I had a very, very large bird wrapped up screeching beside me as I screamed back."

The glider started twirling in a terrifying freefall. Moss had dropped about 6,700 feet and had only 1,500 feet left before she'd hit the ground. But then the trapped eagle managed to free itself and flew off. With only seconds left before she crashed, Moss sorted out the tangled lines, gained control, and glided to a soft landing.

"I see the eagles quite often and they are incredibly beautiful," Moss told Reuters, "but I must say I have never been so relieved to reach the ground."

MAIL WAIL

A cat named Bat terrorized postal carriers so much that they refused to deliver mail to his owner's house.

The carriers claimed they were afraid of the six-year-old ginger tomcat because he would rake their hands bloody when they shoved the mail through the pet flap in the door. Whenever Bat was outside, he would claw their legs with vicious swipes. The carriers used the pet flap because the house didn't have a mailbox.

In the spring of 2004, Bat's owner, Dan Coyne of Cranbrook, Kent, England, received a letter from the Royal Mail informing him that deliveries to his house had been suspended because of his "guard cat."

The letter, which Coyne shared with the *Sun*, read in part: "The postmen are experiencing problems with your Guard Cat. Sounds ridiculous I know, but as they deliver through the flap the cat scratches them. More incredible than this, your cat has been known to jump on the postmen's leg and dig its claws in."

Coyne told the newspaper, "I can't believe they are scared of him." Then he admitted, "Bat is a bit of a psycho and has been known to launch himself at people. He gets very wound up by the postman and sits under the pet flap waiting for him. As the 'postie' pushes the letters through, I've seen Bat try to swipe him with his claws."

When the London press latched onto the story, the Royal Mail issued a statement claiming it wasn't funny. "Staff safety is paramount."

Coyne had to collect his own mail at the post office until he put up a mailbox by the front gate of his house and kept Bat inside. In an understatement, Coyne said Bat "does get a little stroppy"—British slang for belligerent.

A cat named Dipity may have been inspired by Bat, because she slashed a mail carrier's hand when he was putting letters through a slot in the door. At her home in Huddersfield, England, the cat leaped three feet and clawed him, drawing blood.

The Royal Mail sent her owner, Sarah Gregg, a letter threatening to stop deliveries because the cat was too scary. "I can't say I blame them for threatening to cut me off," Gregg told the *Daily Mirror*. "I love Dipity to bits. She's adorable. But I'd be the first to admit she's a little terror. All she wants to do is pick fights. When I took her to be neutered she tried to gouge lumps out of the vet and was hissing at all the dogs."

CHOWHOUNDS

PRICEY MUNCHIES

Buddy the Labrador retriever enjoyed an expensive snack—two Super Bowl tickets worth $900 apiece.

His owner nearly choked from anger when he found out what Buddy had done.

Just days before the big game between the New York Giants and New England Patriots in 2008, Buddy's owner, Chris Gallagher, was expecting the tickets to be delivered to his home in the Phoenix suburb of Avondale. He had given instructions for the courier to leave the envelope that contained the tickets under the doormat of his home. Instead, while Gallagher was at work, the courier slipped the envelope under the front door.

Buddy chomped, gnawed, nibbled, and swallowed portions of the coveted tickets.

The three-year-old dog had a history of turning Gallagher's things into chew toys—like sunglasses, shoes, and footballs. But munching on Super Bowl tickets for club-level seats on the 30-yard line? That was unforgivable.

When Gallagher returned home that evening and saw the remains of the valuable tickets scattered across the living room floor, he went ballistic. Buddy fled through the doggy door and was forced to stay out in the backyard for the next two nights.

What saved Buddy from worse punishment was that the tickets were replaceable because he hadn't destroyed their barcodes. Rather than have the replacement tickets delivered to the house again, Gallagher arranged to have them waiting at the "will call" window at the University of Phoenix Stadium where the game was played.

"It wasn't funny at the time," Gallagher told the *Arizona Republic*. "He's a troublemaker. But he looks at you with those big eyes and you can't be mad for long. About an hour or two after it happened, I was laughing about it. This is the ultimate 'my dog ate it' story."

Pepper Ann, a black Labrador mix, has chewed her way into more trouble than most dogs. Over the years, she has gnawed on anything within reach, from lipstick to ballpoint pens, from bottles of shampoo to tubes of toothpaste. And don't let her get near a box of tissues.

But all her petty crimes paled in comparison to the costly—and stinky—mess the eight-year-old caused during the summer of 2007.

"She's always been naughty, and when she was little it was 'you're lucky you're so cute or you'd be gone otherwise,'" said her owner Debbie Hulleman of Menomonie, Wisconsin. Talking to Minneapolis–St. Paul station KARE-TV, she added, "But she's just a cute little dog. She has personality, but she has issues also."

Especially chewing on things.

When Hulleman and her husband went on vacation, she asked her mother to care for Pepper Ann and the dog's much better-behaved sibling, Zach. Grandma was given strict instructions to keep anything and everything of value out of Pepper Ann's sight. Unfortunately, Grandma forgot to tell a friend, who came for an overnight visit and left her purse on the floor.

Talk about easy pickings for Pepper Ann. During

the night, she stuck her nose in the woman's purse and was delighted at all the fun things she could chew—including an envelope containing about $750 in cash.

The next morning, Grandma and her friend were in shock. Pieces of greenbacks were scattered all over the house. The women gathered up the remnants, including some that the dog had thrown up. They were able to clean and piece together only about $250 worth of bills.

When Hulleman returned to pick up her dogs and learned what happened, she was afraid she would have to pay the woman for all the chewed-up money that wasn't recovered—about $500. As she fretted over her situation, Hulleman went out to her mother's backyard to clean up the dog droppings. To her surprise, she discovered a $50 bill sticking out from a pile of dog poop. So she carefully examined all the other piles that Pepper Ann had left in the yard . . . and lo and behold she collected a total of $400!

She had to clean each bill and tape some of the torn ones together, but at least $650 had been recovered. They would have salvaged all the money had someone been able to find the other half of a $100 bill. Federal regulations say mutilated currency can be replaced if more than 50 percent of a bill is identifiable.

The Hullemans paid the woman for the $100

that was unrecoverable, knowing that the payout could have been a lot worse. As for Pepper Ann? "She goes from room to room, looking to get into trouble," said Hulleman.

Augie, a greater Swiss mountain dog, was another money-hungry pooch.

His owner, Kelley Davis of Apex, North Carolina, placed $400 in cash on her bedroom dresser. She planned to deposit the money, which came from working overtime shifts as a physical therapist, in the bank the next day in 2009. After she left the room, Augie swiped the bills and ate them all.

When Davis discovered what he had done, she took the two-year-old dog for a long walk, during which he made his own deposits. She found pieces of three $100 bills and five twenties.

Referring to a bowl-shaped strainer normally used to wash foods, Davis grabbed a garden hose and shouted at her two children, "Kids, get the colander. I'm out here panning for gold."

Over the next couple of days Davis was able to clean and piece together most of the money Augie had eaten.

RING-A-DING-A-LING

There was a reason why Mark Meltz couldn't find the ring he was supposed to give to his bride on their wedding day. Their yellow Labrador retriever, Liza, had it—in her stomach.

The day before he was to marry Hillary Feinberg, Meltz of Peabody, Massachusetts, left the gold band on the kitchen counter so he would remember to give it to his brother, who was to be the best man at the wedding in 2000. But on the morning of the big day, Meltz couldn't find the ring. He assumed that his brother had taken it. Nope, said his brother. Meltz racked his brain over what could have happened to it.

He took the couple's one-and-a-half-year-old Lab for a walk as he mulled over what to do. When the dog began making weird coughs, Meltz pieced together a possible scenario: The family cat must have jumped up on the counter, played with the ring, and knocked it to the floor where Liza came by and swallowed it.

On this hunch, the desperate groom-to-be took the dog to Angell Memorial Animal Hospital in Boston, where veterinarian Kathleen Wirth took an X-ray of Liza's stomach. Yep, there was the missing ring. But there was not enough time to extract it before the afternoon wedding.

What to do? Meltz's brother came up with the solution.

When it came time to exchange rings, the bride gave Meltz a wedding ring, and the groom gave her the X-ray of the missing ring. No one else in attendance knew what was happening. "But once I explained it to everyone, they exploded with laughter," Meltz told the *Boston Herald*. Lucky for him, Hillary broke into laughter instead of tears.

Rather than operate on Liza, the Meltzes decided to let nature take its course.

While the newlyweds headed to Hawaii for their honeymoon, Meltz's parents kept an eye on Liza, expecting her to give up the ring in the traditional doggy way. Instead, Liza threw up, and out came the ring right onto the Meltzes' clean rug.

HOT DOG

Skylar was one of those dogs who love to "counter surf"—snatch food off the kitchen counter or table. Sometimes she got lucky and scored a ham sandwich or a cookie. Sometimes she got caught and was reprimanded.

And one time, she got really unlucky and nearly burned down the house.

Skylar was a mischievous three-year-old golden-doodle—a golden retriever/poodle mix—who lived with her owner, Fred L. "Chip" Haines IV, in a house in Naperville, Illinois.

One April morning in 2006, Haines was running late for his real-estate job. "I didn't do my typical sweep through the kitchen to make sure Skylar couldn't get at anything," Haines told the *Daily Herald*.

He forgot about the leftover pieces of frozen pizza he had baked for dinner the night before. He left the four center squares still on top of the cardboard tray that had come in the pizza packaging. The cardboard was sitting over the stove's right front and back burners.

Although Haines didn't notice the leftover pizza, Skylar did. Shortly after her owner left for work, the dog tried to steal the remaining slices. She jumped up against the stove, but the food was just out of her reach, so she tried a few more times. On one of her attempts, her paw struck the easy-to-operate control knob on the front of the stove and turned on one of the right burners.

The burner ignited the cardboard and pizza, producing flames that spread quickly to a nearby, heavy-duty plastic cutting board and then onto the cabinets above the stove.

Seeing smoke coming from the kitchen, a neighbor

called 911. Naperville firefighters raced to the scene and broke down a door after learning Skylar was trapped inside. They found the dog unconscious from smoke inhalation on the floor of the living room, scooped her up, and rushed her outdoors. Paramedics strapped a mask to Skylar's snout and used two bottles of oxygen to try to revive her. It took ten minutes before she lifted her head and started wagging her tail.

"Skylar's fur is white, but when I saw her that day, she was literally a black dog" from the fire's soot and ash, Haines said. A bath restored Skylar's natural color.

Naperville fire investigators concluded that the pizza-loving, counter-surfing dog had started the blaze, which had turned the kitchen into cinders. Damage was estimated at $50,000.

Skylar and Haines temporarily moved in with a friend. But despite the fire she caused and her brush with death, the dog just couldn't resist continually jumping onto the kitchen counter and stealing food.

AH-CHEW!

Sunshine the golden retriever tore apart any chance that a student would leave the country on a long-anticipated school trip—by chewing on the teen's passport.

In June 2009, Jon Meier, 17, of Eau Claire, Wisconsin, was getting ready to go with his high school Spanish class to Peru for 12 days. While packing, Jon put his passport in the pouch of a waistband designed to be worn inside a shirt to guard against pickpockets. He placed the waistband on a table and continued preparing for the trip. Meanwhile, when no one was looking, his one-year-old dog snatched the waistband off the table, pulled out the passport, and began gnawing on it.

Twenty minutes before Jon was set to leave home, he discovered that Sunshine had mutilated the vitally important document. "He had chewed a little bit off the corner," said the senior at North High School. "The only thing you could not see was a few numbers. Other than that it was pretty much intact."

He didn't think it would be a problem so he joined his fellow students on a bus that took them to Chicago O'Hare International Airport. He showed his damaged passport to the gate agent, who cleared him for the flight to Miami where the class was scheduled to take a connecting flight to Lima, Peru.

"In Miami, we started to board, and they wouldn't let me on," Jon told the *Ledger-Telegram*. Officials explained to him that if he left the country with the damaged passport, he would have a difficult time trying to get back into the United States. No amount of pleading by his teacher could convince them otherwise, and it was too late to process a new passport. The disappointed teen took a flight back to Chicago while the rest of his classmates flew on to Peru.

Although he missed out on a trip of a lifetime, Jon said he wasn't angry at Sunshine because, "I love her too much."

PIE-EYED

A little lapdog named Charlie nearly ruined a meat-pie–eating contest by wolfing down 20 pies meant for an upcoming competition.

The dog's appetite caused plenty of ulcers for his owner and the organizers of the fifteenth Annual World Pie Eating Contest in Wigan, England, in 2007.

Dave Williams, the 1995 pie-eating champion, was storing the specially prepared four-and-a-half-inch-wide, single-serving meat pies at his home the day before the big event. As he opened the refrigerator door to remove the pies, he was distracted by a pigeon that flew into his chimney. While Williams was trying to free the bird in the other room, Charlie, an eight-year-old bichon frise, raided the refrigerator because the door hadn't been shut tightly enough.

He scarfed down pie after pie, stopping only when his master returned to the kitchen and nearly fainted at the sight. Charlie had devoured 20 meat pies and had stuck his paws in another ten. "I was horrified," Williams told the *Daily Mirror*. "Charlie likes pies, so he probably thought they were for him. I only turned my back for ten minutes and they'd gone."

Williams feared that the contest would be canceled because of Charlie's gluttony, but master pie maker Rob Stewart of Wigan Pies came to the rescue. He worked through the night baking a new batch in time for the event.

Rather than banish Charlie to the doghouse, contest organizers allowed him to compete because they were impressed with his eating skills. Besides, there were no rules barring dogs from entering.

In the past, contestants were judged on the number of pies they consumed in three minutes, but because of new healthy-eating programs, the contest was changed to how fast one pie could be consumed. For the 2007 event, the winner set a record, swallowing all of his pie in 34 seconds. Apparently, Charlie was still too full from the night before. The only nonhuman competitor didn't even finish his pie.

Williams said he forgave his dog for gorging himself on the pies. "Charlie was a rescued dog and had a habit of picking food off the street. We think this trait has stuck with him because he never knew where his next meal was coming from as a youngster, so there was no way we could be angry at him for eating all the pies."

FISH TALE

A young female seal broke into a Massachusetts state fish hatchery and dined on an all-you-can-eat trout buffet before she was captured and returned to the ocean.

In January 2009, the seal left Cape Cod Bay and traveled over land for nearly two miles. She had to waddle across the Sandwich Boardwalk, go through a tunnel under a highway, follow a creek that passes by a mini-golf course, and journey through a wooded area to reach the hatchery's fish-filled lagoons. Obviously having built up a huge appetite from her journey, she chose the one lagoon that held the largest trout, most weighing four pounds or more. No one was sure how many fish she ate.

The three-foot-long, seven-month-old seal was discovered when Division of Fisheries and Wildlife employees made their regular morning rounds. Hatchery manager Craig Lodowsky told the *Cape Cod Times* that it was the first time any of them ever saw a seal dining in the hatchery. Although seals live and breed in salt water, they can spend short periods of time in freshwater.

"It's either a very smart little seal or a very lucky little seal," said Katie Touhey, a spokeswoman for the Cape Cod Stranding Network, which assists stranded marine mammals. As the little seal surfaced with a foot-long trout clenched between her teeth, Touhey said, "It looks healthy enough, pretty full in fact."

Hatchery employees and stranding experts captured the seal with a net and examined her before putting her into a large animal carrier and driving 20 miles to West Dennis Beach along Nantucket Sound, where the seal was eventually released. Before she was freed, they measured, tagged, and painted fluorescent green dye on her snout and torso—all aimed at identifying her if she returned to the hatchery, where she was certainly not welcome.

TABLE SERVICE

A mama bear and her two cubs were so hungry that they walked into a restaurant and began eating the food left behind by customers, who fled in terror.

The 350-pound brown bear and her young ones lapped up the unfinished meals at a diner in Sinaia, Romania, in the summer of 2008. After cleaning their plates, the three bears raided the kitchen and began helping themselves to more food.

"It was like 'Goldilocks and the Three Bears' in reverse," customer Flaviu Lazar told reporters. "But this time they wanted the whole menu, not just porridge."

The hungry animals left before police and local wildlife authorities could track them down. No one was injured.

"We are used to bears sometimes coming into the town at night from the nearby forests as they look for food left out in bins," said Lazar. "But no one had ever seen anything like this."

The year before, a wolf strolled into a packed bar in Villetta Barrea, Italy, helped itself to a steak sandwich from a table, and then walked out again while stunned customers looked on in amazement.

"It sounds like the start of a bad joke, but it really happened," bar owner Giacinto Lorenzo told the press. He said the wolf probably came from the nearby Abruzzo National Park. "It looked pretty thin and we guess it must have been suffering with the recent cold weather and the snow.

"Everyone was so frightened we couldn't move for about five minutes afterwards, but the wolf just sauntered out as if it was the most normal thing in the world."

ROAD RAIDER

An elephant too lazy to search for food in the wild found a much easier way to fill its stomach—by resorting to highway robbery.

Motorists in northern Keonjhar district of Orissa in eastern India complained to authorities in 2007 that a pachyderm would step out into the middle of the road and refuse to let their vehicles pass unless they gave it food.

Witnesses told the *Hindustan Times* that the elephant was scouting for food on the highway, forcing motorists to roll down their windows and get out of their vehicles. "The tusker inserts its trunk inside the vehicle and sniffs for food," Prabodh Mohanty, who had two encounters with the elephant, told the newspaper. "If you are carrying vegetables and bananas inside your vehicle, then it will gulp them and allow you to go."

But if the motorist failed to lower his window or resisted opening the vehicle door, the pachyderm would push the vehicle and stand right in front of it until the driver allowed him to carry out its routine check.

Forest officials said the elephant was old and looking for easy food. "We are telling commuters regularly not to tease the elephant," said Sirish Mohanty, a forest ranger. "So far it has not harmed anybody."

SWEET-TEMPERED

Koni, the Labrador retriever owned by Russian Prime Minister Vladimir Putin, never passed up an opportunity to grab a bite—even when the food was meant for officials at an important political meeting.

Putin had invited leaders of the United Russia party to meet with him at his residence in Novo-Ogaryovo outside of Moscow to discuss ways to help the local food industry. While the meeting got under way, servants were setting up a table in the next room with pastries, biscuits, and jellied desserts.

When the room was unoccupied, Koni sneaked in and, acting like a canine vacuum cleaner, cleaned the table of all the goodies.

"Koni ate everything," said one of Putin's astounded bodyguards.

What Putin said after learning what Koni had done was kept classified.

ABOUT THE AUTHOR

Allan Zullo is the author of nearly 100 nonfiction books on subjects ranging from sports and the supernatural to history and animals.

He has written the bestselling Haunted Kids series, published by Scholastic, which are filled with chilling stories based on or inspired by documented cases from the files of ghost hunters. Allan also has introduced Scholastic readers to the Ten True Tales series, about people who have met the challenges of dangerous, sometimes life-threatening situations. He is the author of such animal books as *Incredible Dogs and Their Incredible Tales*, *True Tales of Animal Heroes*, and *Surviving Sharks and Other Dangerous Creatures*.

Allan, the grandfather of five and the father of two grown daughters, lives with his wife, Kathryn, on the side of a mountain near Asheville, North Carolina. To learn more about the author, visit his Web site at www.allanzullo.com.